Primeros Sonidos

Hortensia y Héctor

Cathy Camarena, M.Ed., and Gloria B. Ruff, M.Ed.

Consulting Editors

Lourdes Flores-Hanson, M.S.E., and Gloria Rosso-White

ABDO
Publishing Company

Published by ABDO Publishing Company, 4940 Viking Drive, Edina, Minnesota 55435.

Printed in the United States.

Credits
Curriculum Coordinator: Nancy Tuminelly
Cover and Interior Design and Production: Mighty Media
Child Photography: Steven Wewerka, Wewerka Photography
Photo Credits: AbleStock, Brand X Pictures, Comstock

Library of Congress Cataloging-in-Publication Data

Camarena, Cathy, 1966-
    Hortensia y Héctor / Cathy Camarena, Gloria B. Ruff.
        p. cm. -- (Primeros sonidos)
    ISBN 1-59679-873-4 (hardcover)
    ISBN 1-59679-874-2 (paperback)
    1. Spanish language--Consonants--Juvenile literature. I. Ruff, Gloria B., 1971-
II. Title. III. Series.
    PC4159.C3575 2006
    468.1'3--dc22

                                                                        2005053651

SandCastle™ books are created by a professional team of educators, reading specialists, and content developers around five essential components that include phonemic awareness, phonics, vocabulary, text comprehension, and fluency. All books are written, reviewed, and leveled for guided and early intervention reading, and designed for use in shared, guided, and independent reading and writing activities to support a balanced approach to literacy instruction.

Let Us Know

After reading the book, SandCastle would like you to tell us your stories about reading. What is your favorite page? Was there something hard that you needed help with? Share the ups and downs of learning to read. We want to hear from you! To get posted on the ABDO Publishing Company Web site, send us e-mail at:

sandcastle@abdopub.com

SandCastle Level: Beginning

ABCChDEFGH
IJKLLLMNÑOP
QRSTUVWXYZ

abcchdefgh
ijklllmnñop
qrstuvwxyz

Hortensia

Héctor

huevo

hormiga

hacha

helado

hoja

Es un   .

Es una .

Es un .

Es .

Es una .

16

Hortensia tiene un huevo.

El huevo es blanco.

Héctor ve una hormiga.

La hormiga es grande.

La hormiga suelta el huevo.

El huevo está en la mesa.

¿Cuáles de estas cosas comienzan con h?

Más palabras que comienzan con h

hada

halcón

helicóptero

hielo

hombre

About SandCastle™

A professional team of educators, reading specialists, and content developers created the SandCastle™ series to support young readers as they develop reading skills and strategies and increase their general knowledge. The SandCastle™ series has four levels that correspond to early literacy development in young children. The levels are provided to help teachers and parents select the appropriate books for young readers.

Emerging Readers
(no flags)

Beginning Readers
(1 flag)

Transitional Readers
(2 flags)

Fluent Readers
(3 flags)

These levels are meant only as a guide. All levels are subject to change.

ABDO
Publishing Company

To see a complete list of SandCastle™ books and other nonfiction titles from ABDO Publishing Company, visit **www.abdopub.com** or contact us at:
4940 Viking Drive, Edina, Minnesota 55435 • 1-800-800-1312 • fax: 1-952-831-1632